AN IRISH WOMAN'S
Book of Days

Compiled by Elizabeth Golding

Gill & Macmillan

This book was designed and produced for
Gill & Macmillan
by Teapot Press Ltd

Compiled by Elizabeth Golding
Edited by Fiona Biggs
Designed by Tony Potter

Gill & Macmillan
Hume Avenue, Park West,
Dublin 12
with associated companies
throughout the world
www.gillmacmillanbooks.ie

ISBN: 978-0-7171-5484-5

Printed in Slovenia

A GIFT FOR

. . . .

FROM

. . . .

January

Eanáir

JANUARY ❖ EANÁIR

❊ 1 ❊

1973 *Ireland joins the European Economic Community along with Britain and Denmark*

❊ 2 ❊

Yet backed by nature I can tell each feature, of this lovely creature called the Star of Slane
'The Star of Slane'

❊ 3 ❊

1925 *Maureen Potter, Irish actress and comedienne, is born*

❊ 4 ❊

Her speech is like music, so sweet and so free
'The Geraldine's Daughter', J. C. Mangan

❊ 5 ❊

1869 *Birth of Margaret Tennant, Irish social work pioneer*

❊ 6 ❊

Little Christmas (Nollaig Bheag), or Women's Christmas (Nollaig na mBan), is one of the traditional names in Ireland for 6 January, more commonly known in the rest of the world as the Feast of the Epiphany

---

❊ 7 ❊

May we have the grace of God and may we die in Ireland
Irish blessing

My guiding star of hope you are, all glow and grace.

J. C. Mangan

❀ 8 ❀

Millions of hearts are thine
'Eire a Rúin'

❀ 9 ❀

2012 *Death of Bridget 'Bridie' Gallagher (The Girl from Donegal), singer*

❀ 10 ❀

1922 *Arthur Griffith is elected president of the Irish Free State*

❀ 11 ❀

1942 *Muriel Day born in Newtownards, Co. Down, the first singer from Northern Ireland to represent Ireland in the Eurovision Song Contest*

❀ 12 ❀

1930 *Birth of Jennifer Johnston, novelist and playwright, in Dublin*

❀ 13 ❀

I wear a shamrock in my heart
'Shamrocks', Rosa Mulholland

❀ 14 ❀

A good heart never went to hell
Irish proverb

Not a passing cloud should darken the sunshine of today

Ellen Mary Downing

JANUARY ❖ EANÁIR

❀ 15 ❀
2006 *Death of Mella Carroll, the first woman to serve as a judge of the Irish High Court*

❀ 16 ❀
1816 *Birth of Frances Browne, Irish poet and storyteller*

❀ 17 ❀
I've sought by every way her heart to gain
'Pearl of the White Breast', G. Petrie

❀ 18 ❀
1822 *Opening of the Theatre Royal, Dublin*

❀ 19 ❀
1787 *Birth of Mary Aikenhead, founder of the Irish Sisters of Charity and St Vincent's Hospital, Dublin*

❀ 20 ❀
1980 *Birth of Lucinda Creighton TD*

❀ 21 ❀
1933 *Death of George Moore, Irish novelist*

But when he came courting beneath our old tree,
His voice was like music – my cushla machree

My Connor

✦ 22 ✦

1967 *Birth of Eleanor McEvoy, Irish singer-songwriter*

✦ 23 ✦

1859 *Kathleen Tynan, writer and poet, born in Clondalkin, Co. Dublin*

✦ 24 ✦

1890 *Birth of Geraldine Cummins, Irish novelist and playwright*

✦ 25 ✦

The truth is rarely pure, and never simple
Oscar Wilde

✦ 26 ✦

1907 *John Millington Synge's* Playboy of the Western World *opens to riots at the Abbey Theatre, Dublin*

✦ 27 ✦

1944 *Mairead Corrigan Maguire, Northern Ireland peace campaigner and Nobel Prize winner, is born*

✦ 28 ✦

1939 *Death of William Butler Yeats, Irish poet*

I'd freely die to save her, And think my lot divine

My Land, T. Davis

January ❖ Eanáir

❀ 29 ❀

To you belongs the empire of the heart
Thomas Dermody

❀ 30 ❀

1845 *Birth of Kitty O'Shea, English mistress and later wife of Charles Stewart Parnell*

❀ 31 ❀

No shadow of falsehood to cloud his blue eyes
'Mo Bhuachaillín Bán', Ralph Varian

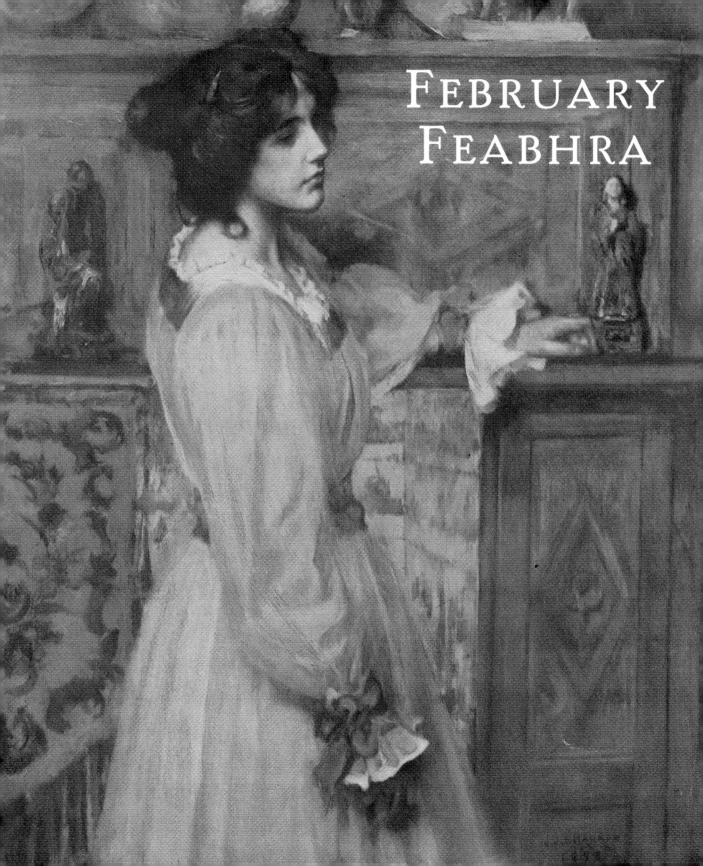

February

Feabhra

FEBRUARY ❖ FEABHRA

—— 1 ——

Feast of St Brigid, female patron of Ireland

—— 2 ——

1882 *James Joyce is born in Dublin*

—— 3 ——

1896 *Death of Lady Jane Wilde, who wrote under the pseudonym 'Speranza'*

—— 4 ——

1865 *Maud Gonne MacBride, Irish revolutionary, is born*

—— 5 ——

1921 *Death of Kitty O'Shea, wife of Irish leader Charles Stewart Parnell*

—— 6 ——

Never take a wife who has no fault
Old Irish saying

—— 7 ——

1992 *The Maastricht Treaty is signed by 12 nations, creating the European Union*

Cheeks bright as the rose – feet light as the doe's

Kitty Neil, John F. Waller

FEBRUARY ❖ FEABHRA

🌿 8 🌿

1926 *First performance of Sean O'Casey's* The Plough and the Stars, *at the Abbey Theatre, leading to riots three nights later*

🌿 9 🌿

1923 *Irish playwright Brendan Behan is born in Dublin*

🌿 10 🌿

1800 *The House of Lords in London votes for the Act of Union, which sees Ireland lose its own parliament*

🌿 11 🌿

1896 *Oscar Wilde's play* Salomé *opens in Paris at the Théâtre de l'Oeuvre, while the playwright is in prison*

🌿 12 🌿

1981 *Lisa Hannigan, Irish singer, songwriter and musician, is born*

🌿 13 🌿

1827 *Birth of Sister Julia McGroarty, Irish founder of Trinity College, Washington DC*

🌿 14 🌿

Day dedicated to St Valentine, whose remains are enshrined in Whitefriar Street Church, Dublin

And a radiance, like a glory, beamed
in the light she left behind her

Aileen, J. C. Mangan

February ❖ Feabhra

❦ 15 ❧
1971 *Irish currency changes to the decimal system*

❦ 16 ❧
But that doth rest between thy breast, A heart of purest core
'Brighdín Bán Mo Stór', E. Walsh

❦ 17 ❧
1945 *Academy award-winning actress Brenda Fricker is born in Dublin*

❦ 18 ❧
1948 *Birth of Irish actress Sinéad Cusack*

❦ 19 ❧
Taste is the feminine of genius
Edward Fitzgerald

❦ 20 ❧
2009 *Christy Nolan, Whitbread award-winning Irish writer, dies*

❦ 21 ❧
2009 *Over 100,000 people protest in Dublin over the financial and banking crisis affecting Ireland*

In thee my life of life yet lies

The Karamanian Exile, J. C. Mangan

February · Feabhra

22
1832 *First burial in Glasnevin Cemetery, Dublin*

23
1943 *Thirty-five orphan girls die in a fire at St Joseph's Orphanage, Cavan Town*

24
Both your friend and your enemy think you will never die
Irish proverb

25
1570 *Pope Pius V issues the bull* Regnans in Excelsis, *declaring Elizabeth I of England a heretic and releasing her subjects from any allegiance to her*

26
And you the hope, voice, battle-axe, the shield of us and ours
'Shaun's Head', John Savage

27
1981 *Birth of Yvonne Tracy, Irish international footballer*

28
1938 *Birth of Alice Taylor, Irish writer*

There's no flower that e'er bloomed can my rose excel

The Little Black Rose, Thomas Furlong

❖ 29 ❖

*Leap Year, a year containing one additional day in order to keep the calendar
year synchronised with the astronomical or seasonal year*

March
Márta

MARCH ❖ MÁRTA

1

1940 *Birth of Nuala O'Faolain, journalist and writer (d. 2008)*

2

It is not a fish until it is on the bank
Irish proverb

3

1977 *Birth of Ronan Keating, pop star who set up the Marie Keating Foundation
to promote breast cancer awareness*

4

My aims are not ambitious, and my wishes are but small
'The Old Plaid Shawl', Francis A. Fahy

5

In Carlow town there lived a maid, More sweet than flowers at daybreak
'The Carlow Maid'

6

1918 *Death of Irish nationalist leader John Redmond*

7

1920 *Irish novelist Eilis Dillon is born*

The last snow melts upon bush and bramble,
The gold bars shine on the forest's floor

Aubrey de Vere

March ❖ Márta

8

1966 *Irish republicans blow up Nelson's Pillar in O'Connell Street, Dublin*

9

1973 *Northern Ireland votes in a referendum to remain within the United Kingdom*

10

1967 *Death of Ina Boyle, Irish composer*

11

1812 *Musician and opera composer William Vincent Wallace is born in Waterford*

12

If you're the only one that knows you're afraid, you're brave
Irish proverb

13

1944 *Great Britain suspends all travel between Ireland and the UK to prevent German spies learning war secrets*

14

1778 *Robert Emmet, Irish revolutionary, is born*

Full of health and heart

J. C. Mangan

MARCH ❖ MÁRTA

❦ 15 ❦

1852 *Birth of Lady Gregory, playwright, folklorist and co-founder of the Abbey Theatre*

❦ 16 ❦

Ignorance is a heavy burden
Irish proverb

❦ 17 ❦

2012 *Mayo-born Mae Collins, who emigrated to the United States in 1922, celebrates her 107th birthday by riding in an open-top convertible in the St Patrick's Day parade in New York*

❧ 18 ❧

1792 *Death of Arabella Denny, Irish philanthropist and founder of the first Magdalene asylum*

❧ 19 ❧

A misty winter brings a pleasant spring; a pleasant winter, a misty spring
Traditional saying

❧ 20 ❧

1964 *Playwright and novelist Brendan Behan dies in Dublin*

❧ 21 ❧

1970 *Dana (Rosemary Brown) wins the Eurovision Song Contest for Ireland, for the first time*

The primrose of Ireland, for wheresoe'er I go

Irish Molly, street ballad

MARCH ❖ MÁRTA

❧ 22 ❧
1848 *Birth of Sarah Purser, Irish artist*

❧ 23 ❧
1947 *Former Irish politician Liz McManus is born in Canada*

❧ 24 ❧
1909 *Death of Irish playwright and poet John Millington Synge*

MARCH ❖ MÁRTA

❦ 25 ❧
1738 *Death of Irish harpist and composer Turlough O'Carolan*

❦ 26 ❧
I love conversation, likewise recreation
'Nice Little Jane', street ballad

❦ 27 ❧
1650 *The Siege of Kilkenny ends with surrender to Oliver Cromwell*

❦ 28 ❧
1824 *Death of Catherine Wilmot, Irish traveller and diarist*

❦ 29 ❧
2004 *Smoking is banned in all work places in Ireland*

❦ 30 ❧
1880 *Birth of Irish playwright Seán O'Casey*

❦ 31 ❧
1872 *Arthur Griffith is born in Dublin*

Sly little cupid has knocked me stupid

Hannah Healy, street ballad

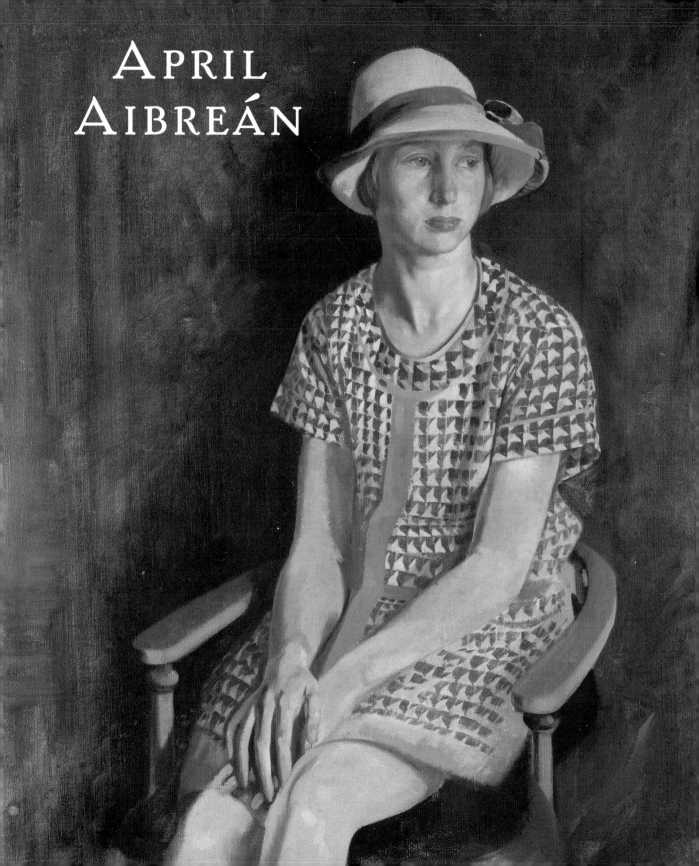

APRIL
AIBREÁN

APRIL ❖ AIBREÁN

1

1911 *Launch of the luxury liner* Titanic *from the Harland & Wolff shipyard, Belfast*

2

1902 *Maud Gonne stars in the first production of Yeats'* Cathleen ni Houlihan

3

1900 *Oldest surviving moving film in Ireland shows Queen Victoria's last visit to Dublin*

4

1951 *Birth of Adele King (Twink), popular singer and actress*

5

1869 *Birth of Margaret Tennant, Irish pioneer in social work*

6

May we have the grace of God and may we die in Ireland
Irish blessing

7

I would walk the dew with you, and the desert of the plains
J. C. Mangan

And my soul within is love for you,
and that neither of yesterday nor today

J. C. Mangan

APRIL ❖ AIBREÁN

❀ 8 ❀

Rich in all women's loveliness
'The Fire-Worshippers', Tom Moore

❀ 9 ❀

1913 *Death of Irish-born barrister, Sir Henry John Wrixon, campaigner for female suffrage*

❀ 10 ❀

1940 *Gloria Hunniford, television and radio presenter, is born in Portadown, Co. Armagh*

❀ 11 ❀

1878 *Birth of Kathleen Clark, revolutionary, senator and lord mayor of Dublin*

 To thy door by love lighted, I first saw those eyes

Desmond's Song, Tom Moore

————— ❧ 12 ❧ —————

1737 *Irish actress Margaret Woffington plays Ophelia at Smock Alley Theatre, Dublin*

————— ❧ 13 ❧ —————

1742 *Première of Handel's* Messiah *in Fishamble Street, Dublin*

————— ❧ 14 ❧ —————

1859 *Death of Irish novelist Sydney Owenson, Lady Morgan*

And she is the flower of Munster, she, my Róisín Dubh

J. C. Mangan

❧ 15 ❧

1912 *At 2.20 am the* Titanic *sinks, with the loss of 1,514 lives*

❧ 16 ❧

1941 *Belfast suffers a Nazi bombing raid*

❧ 17 ❧

1969 *Bernadette McAliskey (née Devlin) wins the Mid-Ulster by-election at the age of 21, becoming the youngest ever female MP at Westminster*

❧ 18 ❧

1949 *The Republic of Ireland Act comes into force and the Republic of Ireland leaves the British Commonwealth*

❧ 19 ❧

A woman can beat the devil
Irish proverb

❧ 20 ❧

1946 *Death of Hannah Sheehy-Skeffington, founding member of the Irish Women Workers' Union*

❧ 21 ❧

1902 *Death of Ethna Corby (née Anne Johnston), journalist, poet, nationalist and founding member of Inghinidhe na hÉireann*

And where you go we'll follow, with you to stand or fall!

The Blacksmith of Limerick, R.D. Joyce

April ❖ Aibreán

❀ 22 ❀

1894 *Birth of Irish stained glass artist Evie Hone*

❀ 23 ❀

1014 *The defeat of Mael Mórdha mac Murchada and the Viking forces by the armies of Brian Boru marks the beginning of the decline of Viking power in Ireland*

❀ 24 ❀

1916 *Easter Rising: The Irish Republican Brotherhood leads an action to seize key government buildings in Dublin, and issues the* Proclamation of the Irish Republic

APRIL ❖ AIBREÁN

❦ 25 ❧
1916 *7,000 troops move into Dublin from Belfast following the Proclamation*

❦ 26 ❧
1979 *Grainne Cronin, Aer Lingus's first female pilot, makes her maiden flight for the airline to Frankfurt*

❦ 27 ❧
1953 *Death of Maud Gonne MacBride, Irish revolutionary*

April ❖ Aibreán

28

There was comfort ever on your lip, and the kind look on your brow
'Lament of the Irish Emigrant', Lady Dufferin

29

1916 *The leader of the Easter Rising orders his followers to surrender*

30

1994 Riverdance *is performed for the first time during the interval of the 1994 Eurovision Song Contest in Dublin*

MAY
BEALTAINE

MAY ❖ BEALTAINE

❧ 1 ❧

1891 *Opening of the Dublin Loopline railway bridge*

❧ 2 ❧

1858 *Birth of Edith Somerville, Irish artist and writer*

❧ 3 ❧

1916 *The first of the 1916 rebels are executed after being found guilty of taking part 'in an armed rebellion'*

❧ 4 ❧

1916 *Grace Gifford marries Joseph Mary Plunkett in Kilmainham Gaol, hours before his execution by the British authorities*

❧ 5 ❧

1956 *Irish singer Mary Coughlan is born in Galway*

❧ 6 ❧

1728 *Catholics in Ireland lose the right to vote*

❧ 7 ❧

1915 *The Cunard liner* Lusitania, *bound for Liverpool, is sunk off the Irish coast by a German submarine, with the loss of almost 1,200 lives*

A woman like a lamb, a quiet friendly woman

Irish proverb

MAY ❖ BEALTAINE

8

1916 *Execution of Éamonn Ceannt, born in Galway in 1881*

9

1919 Ann Butler Yeats, painter, stage designer and daughter of Jack B. Yeats, is born in Dublin (d. 4 July 2001)

10

2010 Writer Siobhán Parkinson (b.1954) is conferred as first Laureate na nÓg by then president Mary McAleese

11

1954 Birth of Jane Morrice, former politician in Northern Ireland

12

1712 Building begins on Trinity College Library

13

Soon upon her native strand doth a lovely lady stand
'O'Carolan's Love Song – Bridget Cruise'

14

1915 Birth of Mary Delaney, Irish writer

'Tis in your eyes, my sweetest love!
My only words I see

Nay, do not Weep, T. Moore

MAY ❖ BEALTAINE

🌿 15 🌿

1847 *Daniel O'Connell, Irish political leader, dies in Genoa*

🌿 16 🌿

A soul, too, more than half divine
'The Fire-Worshippers', Tom Moore

🌿 17 🌿

2011 *Queen Elizabeth II arrives in Dublin at the beginning of her first state visit
to the Republic of Ireland*

🌿 18 🌿

2006 *Michael O'Riordan, founder of the Communist Party of Ireland, dies aged 88*

🌿 19 🌿

1882 *Birth of Mary Hayden, Irish historian and campaigner for women's rights*

🌿 20 🌿

A child may have too much of her mother's blessing
Irish proverb

🌿 21 🌿

1945 *Mary Robinson, first female president of Ireland, is born in Ballina, County Mayo*

To praise her beauty then is my duty

The Star of Slane, street ballad

MAY ❖ BEALTAINE

22

1932 *Death of Augusta, Lady Gregory*

23

1903 *Birth of Shelah Richards, Irish actress and director*

24

1923 *Éamon de Valera and Frank Aiken call an end to the Irish Civil War*

25

1895 *Oscar Wilde is convicted in London of gross indecency*

26

It is not a secret if known by three people
Irish proverb

27

1936 *The inaugural Aer Lingus flight takes off from Baldonnel Airport, near Dublin*

28

1929 *Death of Alice Stopford Green, Irish historian and author*

She has a great store of riches and a large sum of gold

The Streams of Bunclody, street ballad

MAY ❖ BEALTAINE

❀ 29 ❀

1884 *Constance Mary Lloyd marries Oscar Wilde*

❀ 30 ❀

1986 *Official opening of Connacht Regional Airport at Knock, Co. Mayo, now Ireland West Airport*

❀ 31 ❀

1937 *Birth of Mary O'Rourke, Irish politician*

JUNE
MEITHEAMH

JUNE ❖ MEITHEAMH

1

It's easy to halve the potato where there's love
Irish proverb

2

1986 *Birth of Katie Taylor, footballer and world champion boxer*

3

1878 *Birth of Sinéad Flanagan, wife of Éamon de Valera*

4

1864 *Birth of Ellen Lucy O'Brien (Neilí Ní Bhrian), Gaelic Leaguer and ecumenist*

5

2005 *Grania Willis becomes the first Irishwoman to reach the summit of the north face of Mount Everest*

6

Good luck comes in trickles; ill luck comes in torrents
Irish proverb

7

1889 *Birth of Elizabeth Bowen, Irish novelist and short story writer*

Oh! Look not so – beneath the skies
I now fear nothing but those eyes

The Fire-Worshippers, Tom Moore

JUNE ❖ MEITHEAMH

 8

1886 *Riots in Belfast follow the defeat of the Home Rule Bill in the House of Commons despite great effort by Prime Minister William Gladstone*

❖ 9 ❖

Better be quarrelling than lonesome
Irish proverb

❖ 10 ❖

1912 *Birth of Irish novelist Mary Lavin*

❖ 11 ❖

1862 *Birth of Violet Florence Martin, who wrote under the pseudonym Martin Ross in collaboration with Edith Somerville*

JUNE ❖ MEITHEAMH

❧ 12 ❧

1932 *Death of Catherine Coll, mother of Éamon de Valera*

❧ 13 ❧

1865 *William Butler Yeats, Irish poet, is born in Dublin*

❧ 14 ❧

Praise youth and it will prosper
Irish proverb

There are some glowing eyes
that leave their living rays behind

Lovely Maryanne, Michael Hogan

June ❖ Meitheamh

❀ 15 ❀

1919 *Pioneer aviators Alcock and Brown crash land a Vickers Vimy aircraft in a bog near Clifden, Co. Galway, to complete the first nonstop transatlantic flight*

❀ 16 ❀

1904 *Nora Barnacle first walks out with James Joyce, and as a tribute he sets the action of* Ulysses *on this date*

❀ 17 ❀

1845 *Irish novelist, poet and historian Emily Lawless is born in Co. Kildare*

❀ 18 ❀

A family of Irish birth will argue and fight, but let a shout come from without and see them all unite
Irish proverb

❀ 19 ❀

1935 *Birth of Mary Holland, Irish political journalist*

❀ 20 ❀

1763 *Birth of Theobald Wolfe Tone, Irish patriot and one of the founding fathers of the United Irishmen*

❀ 21 ❀

1798 *Battle of Vinegar Hill, Enniscorthy, Co. Wexford*

On memory's beaming mirror, in the palace of the mind

Lovely Maryanne, Michael Hogan

JUNE ❖ MEITHEAMH

❧ 22 ❧

1798 *Execution of rebel John Kelly, known to most as 'Kelly, the boy from Killane'*

❧ 23 ❧

1998 *Death in Arizona of Maureen O'Sullivan, the 'first Irish movie star'*

❧ 24 ❧

1874 *Birth of Úna Ní Fhaircheallaigh (Agnes O'Farrelly), Irish feminist, writer and Gaelic Leaguer*

❧ 25 ❧

1891 *Katharine (Kitty) O'Shea marries Charles Stewart Parnell*

❧ 26 ❧

Distant hills look green
Irish proverb

❧ 27 ❧

1846 *Charles Stewart Parnell is born in Avondale, Co. Wicklow*

❧ 28 ❧

The grace of God is found between the saddle and the ground
Irish proverb

I am captivated – I do repeat it –
By Hannah Healy, the pride of Howth

Hannah Healy, street ballad

JUNE ❖ MEITHEAMH

❊ 29 ❊

1985 *U2 play Croke Park, Dublin, for the first time*

❊ 30 ❊

1926 *Death of Eva Gore-Booth, Irish poet and dramatist and sister of Constance Countess Markievicz*

JULY
IÚIL

July ❖ Iúil

❧ 1 ❧
If you go on your travels, may you always come back to Ireland
Irish saying

❧ 2 ❧
1970 *The Irish Catholic hierarchy announces that it is no longer obligatory to abstain from eating meat on Fridays*

❧ 3 ❧
1940 *Bernadette Greevy, Irish mezzo-soprano, is born in Dublin (d. 2008)*

❧ 4 ❧
2012 *New Ross, Co. Wexford, celebrates its first Irish America Day, in recognition of the strong ties between Ireland and the United States*

❧ 5 ❧
1958 *Birth of Veronica Guerin, Irish investigative reporter*

❧ 6 ❧
1939 *Birth of Mary Peters, Irish Olympic athlete*

❧ 7 ❧
1739 *Death of Christian Davies, Irish female soldier, who enlisted in order to find her husband*

She, too, has the soul of an Irish queen

A Lullaby, J. C. Mangan

JULY ❖ IÚIL

❧ 8 ☙

1770 *Birth of Mary Ann McCracken, Irish patriot and philanthropist*

❧ 9 ☙

1959 *Mary Browne becomes the first female member of Garda Síochána na hÉireann*

❧ 10 ☙

1949 *The last ever tram departs from Nelson's Pillar, Dublin*

❧ 11 ☙

1817 *An Act of Parliament establishes the first public lunatic asylums in Ireland*

 12

1796 *The first Orange Order 'Twelfth' demonstration is held*

 13

There is no luck except where there is discipline
Irish proverb

14

1976 *Birth of Kirsten Sheridan, Irish film director and screenwriter*

Sweet and mild would look her face,
O none so sweet and mild

Kathleen Ni Houlahan, J. C. Mangan

JULY ❖ IÚIL

🌸 15 🌸
1927 *Death of Constance Countess Markievicz, revolutionary*

🌸 16 🌸
There is no need like the lack of a friend
Irish proverb

🌸 17 🌸
1884 *Birth of Louise Gavan Duffy, Irish revolutionary and educator*

🌸 18 🌸
1951 *The old Abbey Theatre in Dublin is destroyed by fire*

🌸 19 🌸
1994 *Eilis Dillon, Irish novelist, dies*

🌸 20 🌸
1882 *Death of Fanny Parnell, poet and co-founder of the Ladies' Land League
and sister of Charles Stewart Parnell*

🌸 21 🌸
1975 *Birth of Cara Dillon, Irish folk singer*

I thought her surely a goddess purely,
Or some bright angel in truth I vow

Hannah Healy, street ballad

JULY ❖ IÚIL

❧ 22 ❧
A friend's eye is a good mirror
Irish proverb

❧ 23 ❧
1803 *Robert Emmet's uprising in Dublin begins and ends in a day*

❧ 24 ❧
Your feet will bring you to where your heart is
Irish proverb

❧ 25 ❧
1983 *Birth of Cecelia Joyce, Irish international cricketer*

❧ 26 ❧
1914 *British troops open fire on a crowd at Bachelor's Walk, Dublin, killing four and wounding 37*

❧ 27 ❧
1669 *Christening of Molly Malone, celebrated Irish fishmonger and subject of a famous street ballad*

❧ 28 ❧
1943 *Ten people are killed when a plane crashes on Mount Brandon, Co. Kerry*

A hero shall my bridegroom be

The Fire-Worshippers, Tom Moore

❀ 29 ❀

Your son is your son until he marries, but your daughter is your daughter until you die
Irish proverb

❀ 30 ❀

1680 *Death of Thomas Butler, Earl of Ossory, Irish naval commander*

❀ 31 ❀

1893 *Foundation of the Gaelic League to promote the Irish language*

An angel wise is everyone
That still hath done God's will divine

Anon, 8th–10th century

August
Lúnasa

AUGUST ❖ LÚNASA

❧ 1 ❧
1906 *Opening of Belfast City Hall*

❧ 2 ❧
1849 *State visit to Ireland by Queen Victoria, to Dublin, Belfast and Cork*

❧ 3 ❧
A house is empty and cold without a woman
Irish proverb

❧ 4 ❧
1878 *Birth of Margaret Mary Pearse, Irish senator and sister of Patrick Pearse*

❧ 5 ❧
1934 *Birth of Gay Byrne, Irish broadcaster*

❧ 6 ❧
1830 *First Dublin Horse Show opens*

❧ 7 ❧
1943 *Death of Sarah Purser, Irish artist and founder of a stained glass studio*

Each day I'm declining, in love, I'm repining

Nice Little Jane, street ballad

AUGUST ❖ LÚNASA

✤ 8 ✤

1879 *Birth of Eileen Gray, Irish architect and interior designer*

✤ 9 ✤

1979 *First Vietnamese refugees arrive in Ireland*

✤ 10 ✤

1976 *Peace movement is formed in Belfast after the deaths there of three children*

✤ 11 ✤

One does not tire of a profitable occupation
Irish proverb

I grieve when I think on the dear happy days of my youth

Draherin O Machree, Anon

───── ❧ 12 ❧ ─────

1821 *King George IV arrives in Ireland for a state visit*

───── ❧ 13 ❧ ─────

1974 *Death of Kate O'Brien, Irish dramatist and novelist*

───── ❧ 14 ❧ ─────

1922 *Dublin-born mathematician and philosopher Sophie Willock Bryant dies*

I saw her once, one little while, and then no more

J. C. Mangan

August ❖ Lúnasa

15

1880 *In Derrybeg, Co. Donegal, five massgoers drown when their chapel is flooded*

16

1711 *A medical school and laboratories open at Trinity College Dublin*

17

1921 *Birth of Maureen O'Hara (Maureen Fitzsimmons), Irish film star*

18

You've got to do your own growing, no matter how tall your grandfather was
Irish proverb

19

1869 *Birth of Frank McCourt, Irish writer and Pulitzer prize-winner*

20

Continual cheerfulness is a sign of wisdom
Irish proverb

21

1879 *Apparitions of the Virgin Mary at Knock, Co. Mayo, are seen by at least 22 people*

She casts a spell, oh, casts a spell!

My love, Oh, She is my love, Douglas Hyde

August • Lúnasa

22

1922 *Michael Collins is killed in an ambush by extremist republicans near Bandon, Co. Cork*

23

1999 *Death of James White, Northern Irish writer (b. 1928)*

24

1974 *Birth of Órla Fallon, Irish singer, songwriter and former member of the group* Celtic Woman *and the chamber choir* Anúna

25

1866 *Birth of Susan Mary 'Lily' Yeats, embroiderer and daughter of John Butler Yeats*

26

1913 *First day of the Great Lockout in Dublin, leading to the starvation of 100,000 people by the end of September*

27

1798 *Wolfe Tone's United Irish and French forces clash with the British Army in the Battle of Castlebar, part of the Irish Rebellion of 1798, resulting in the creation of the French puppet Republic of Connaught*

28

1815 *Birth of Mary Martin, Irish novelist*

At the mid hour of night, when stars are weeping, I fly the lone vale we loved, when life shone warm in thine eye

At the Hour of Midnight, Tom Moore

AUGUST ❖ LÚNASA

❀ 29 ❀

1890 *Opening of the National Library of Ireland*

❀ 30 ❀

1951 *Birth of Dana (Rosemary Brown), Irish singer and Eurovision Song Contest winner*

❀ 31 ❀

1869 *Death of Mary Ward, amateur Anglo Irish scientist and world's first known motor vehicle accident victim, killed under the wheels of an experimental steam car*

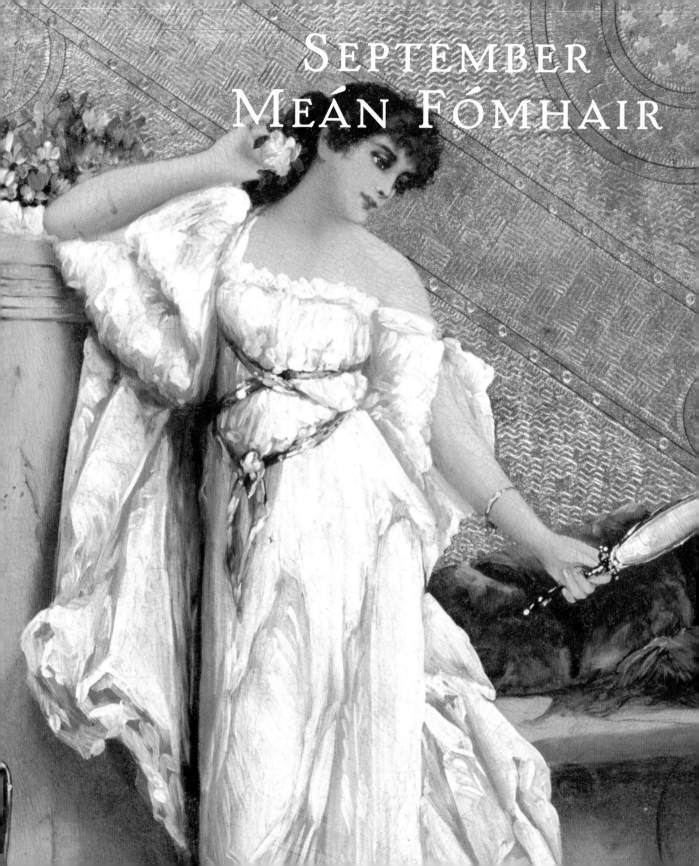

September
MEÁN FÓMHAIR

September ❖ Meán Fómhair

─────────── ❋ 1 ❋ ───────────

1830 *The Dublin Zoological Gardens, third oldest in the world, opens to the public*

─────────── ❋ 2 ❋ ───────────

There is not a tree in heaven higher than the tree of patience
Irish proverb

─────────── ❋ 3 ❋ ───────────

1850 *Establishment of Queen's Colleges in Belfast, Cork and Galway (now Queen's University, University College Cork and University College Galway)*

─────────── ❋ 4 ❋ ───────────

1935 *Birth of Pauline Bewick, Irish artist*

─────────── ❋ 5 ❋ ───────────

1854 *Francis Arthur Fahy, Composer of 'Galway Bay' and 'The Old Plaid Shawl', is born in Kinvara, Co. Galway*

─────────── ❋ 6 ❋ ───────────

1911 *Birth of Lady Angela Christina McDonnell Antrim, Irish sculptor and cartoonist*

─────────── ❋ 7 ❋ ───────────

Where the tongue slips, it speaks the truth
Irish proverb

Dark eyes, wonderful, strange and dear they shone
A moment's space

The Half Door, Seumas O'Sullivan

SEPTEMBER ✦ MEÁN FÓMHAIR

❧ 8 ☙

1908 *St Enda's School opens under the headship of Patrick Pearse*

❧ 9 ☙

1649 *The Siege of Drogheda by Oliver Cromwell's army begins*

❧ 10 ☙

1813 *The 'Limerick Stone', a meteorite weighing over 29kg, falls on Ireland*

❧ 11 ☙

Two-thirds of help is to give courage
Irish proverb

❧ 12 ☙

1907 *Birth of Louis MacNeice, Irish poet (d. 1963)*

❧ 13 ☙

Young people don't know what age is, old people forget what youth was
Irish proverb

❧ 14 ☙

1866 *Birth of Alice Milligan, Irish writer and nationalist*

That angel whose charge was Éire sang thus,
o'er the dark Isle winging

The Three Woes, Aubrey de Vere

September ❖ Meán Fómhair

❧ 15 ☙
1976 *Anne Dickson becomes first female leader of an Irish political party, the*
Unionist Party of Northern Ireland

❧ 16 ☙
1903 *Irish writer Frank O'Connor is born in Cork*

❧ 17 ☙
1934 *Birth of Maureen Connolly (Little Mo), champion Irish-American tennis player*

❧ 18 ☙
1851 *Death of Anne Devlin, Irish heroine and patriot*

❧ 19 ☙
1905 *Death of Dublin-born Thomas Barnardo, philanthropist and founder of homes for poor children*

❧ 20 ☙
1588 *Three ships of the Spanish Armada run aground at Streedagh, Co. Sligo*

❧ 21 ☙
A man is often a bad adviser to himself and a good adviser to another
Irish proverb

He whom a dream hath possessed knoweth no more of doubting

He Whom a Dream Hath Possessed, Shaemas O'Sheel

SEPTEMBER ❖ MEÁN FÓMHAIR

22
1884 HMS Wasp *sinks off Tory Island, with the loss of 52 lives*

23
The only cure for love is marriage
Irish proverb

24
1861 *Opening of Mater Hospital, Dublin*

25
1793 *Birth of the poet Felicia Hemans, who lived in Dublin for the latter part of her life (d. 1835)*

26
1873 *Birth of Anna Smithson, Irish novelist and nurse*

27
The love of God guides every good
Irish proverb

28
1889 *Irish painter Seán (John) Keating is born in Limerick, Dublin (d. 1977)*

Happy the stark bare wood on the hill of Bree!

The Triad of Things Not Decreed, Alice Furlong

September ❖ Meán Fómhair

✳ 29 ✳

1979 *Pope John Paul II addresses a crowd of some 300,000 people in Drogheda, Co. Louth*

✳ 30 ✳

1959 *Première of George Morrison's* Mise Éire *at the Cork Film Festival*

October
Deireadh Fómhair

OCTOBER ❖ DEIREADH FÓMHAIR

✿ 1 ✿

1911 *Unveiling of the Parnell Monument in O'Connell Street, Dublin*

✿ 2 ✿

1942 *A collision between the* Queen Mary *and the cruiser* Curaçao *off the Co. Donegal coast causes the cruiser to sink, with the loss of 338 lives*

✿ 3 ✿

1980 *Miss Justice Mella Carroll becomes the first female judge of the Irish High Court*

✿ 4 ✿

Children begin by loving their parents. After a time they judge them. Rarely, if ever, do they forgive them.
Oscar Wilde

✿ 5 ✿

1911 *Writer and satirist Brian O'Nolan (better known as Flann O'Brien) is born in Strabane, Co. Tyrone*

✿ 6 ✿

1928 *Irish Olympic athlete and hockey player Maeve Kyle is born*

✿ 7 ✿

All women become like their mothers. That is their tragedy. No man does. That's his.
Oscar Wilde

A plenteous place is Ireland for hospitable cheer
Uileacán dubh ó!

The Fair Hills of Ireland, Samuel Ferguson

October ❖ Deireadh Fómhair

❦ 8 ❧
1858 *Birth of Irish novelist Edith Somerville*

❦ 9 ❧
1891 *Pioneering Irish language teacher Lil Nic Dhonnachadha (Lilian Duncan) is born*

❦ 10 ❧
1977 *The Nobel Prize for Peace is awarded to Betty Williams and Mairead Corrigan, founders of the Peace Movement in Northern Ireland*

❦ 11 ❧
1973 *The first Irish female ambassador, Mary Tinney, is appointed to Sweden and Finland*

❦ 12 ❧
1895 *Cecil Frances Alexander, Dublin-born poet and philanthropist, dies*

❦ 13 ❧
1981 *Publication of the first Irish-language version of the Bible for over 200 years*

❦ 14 ❧
1917 *Magdalen Hone, widow of artist Nathaniel Hone, donates a huge collection of paintings to the National Gallery of Ireland*

Mellow the moonlight to shine is beginning

The Spinning Wheel, John Francis Waller

OCTOBER ✦ DEIREADH FÓMHAIR

✿ 15 ✿

1879 *Birth of Sarah Allgood, Irish film actress*

✿ 16 ✿

1854 *Literary genius, raconteur and wit Oscar Wilde is born in Dublin*

✿ 17 ✿

1907 *Guglielmo Marconi starts a telegraph service between Clifden, Co. Galway, and Cape Breton, Canada*

OCTOBER ❖ DEIREADH FÓMHAIR

❧ 18 ☙

1171 *Henry II (1133–89) arrives in Ireland from France and declares himself 'Lord of Ireland'*

❧ 19 ☙

1913 *Death of Emily Lawless, Irish novelist and poet*

❧ 20 ☙

1950 *Birth of Philomena Begley, Irish country singer*

❧ 21 ☙

The lesson learned by a tragedy is a lesson never forgotten
Irish proverb

The closing of an autumn evening is like the running of a hound across the moor

Anon

OCTOBER ❖ DEIREADH FÓMHAIR

❀ 22 ❀

1884 *The first female graduates are conferred by the Royal University of Ireland*

❀ 23 ❀

If wars were fought with words Ireland would be ruling the world
Irish saying

❀ 24 ❀

1880 *The first meeting of the Irish Ladies' Land League, founded by Fanny Parnell, Ellen Ford and Jane Byrne, takes place in New York*

OCTOBER ❖ DEIREADH FÓMHAIR

❄ 25 ❄
1968 *The New University of Coleraine, Ulster, is officially opened*

❄ 26 ❄
Women are stronger than men, they do not die of wisdom
Irish proverb

❄ 27 ❄
2011 *Birth of Peter O'Meara, Irish actor*

❄ 28 ❄
Man to the hills, woman to the shore
Irish proverb

❄ 29 ❄
1825 *Birth of Catherine Hayes, Irish opera singer*

❄ 30 ❄
1997 *Mary McAleese is elected eighth president of the Republic of Ireland*

❄ 31 ❄
1883 *Birth of Irish actress Sarah Allgood*

The grand road from the mountain goes shining to the sea

The Little Waves of Breffny, *Eva Gore-Booth*

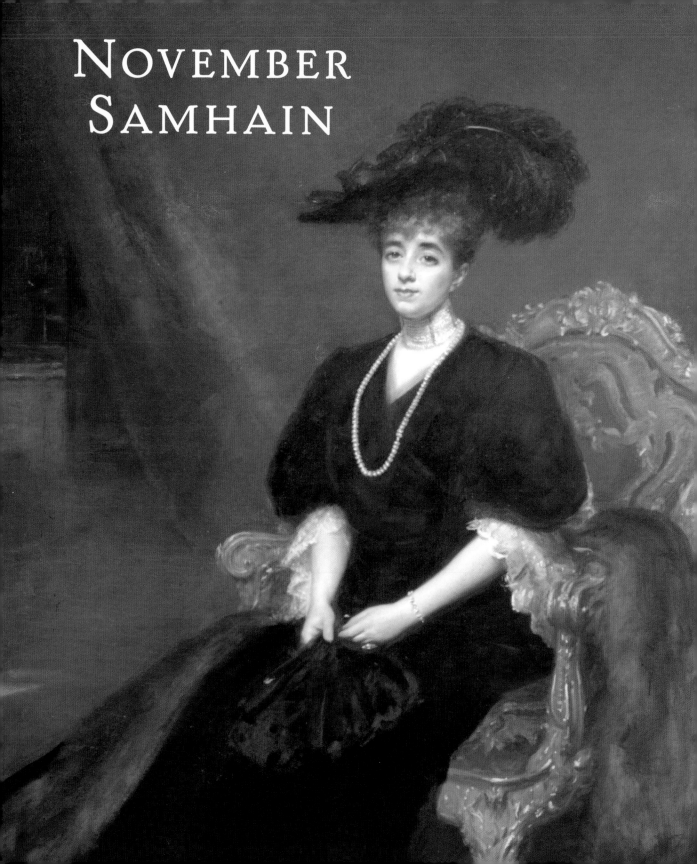

NOVEMBER
SAMHAIN

November ❖ Samhain

1

1884 *Founding of the GAA (Gaelic Athletic Association)*

2

1952 *Death of Irish actress Molly Allgood*

3

1969 *The Irish Republic introduces the breathalyser*

4

Her speech is like music, so sweet and so free
'The Geraldine's Daughter', J. C. Mangan

5

1987 *Death of Irish broadcaster and television personality Eamonn Andrews*

6

Don't bless with the tip of your tongue if there's bile at the butt
Irish saying

7

1968 *A state funeral is held for Senator Margaret Pearse*

One that is ever kind said yesterday
Your well beloved's hair has threads of grey

The Folly of Being Comforted, William Butler Yeats

November ❖ Samhain

❦ 8 ❧

1990 *Mary Robinson is elected first female president of the Republic of Ireland*

❦ 9 ❧

1926 *Irish playwright, author and humorist John Byrne, better known as Hugh Leonard, is born*

❦ 10 ❧

1969 *Karen Corr, professional pool player, is born in Ballymoney, Northern Ireland*

❦ 11 ❧

1841 *Death of Catherine McAuley, Catholic activist and founder of the Sisters of Mercy*

❦ 12 ❧

1798 *Irish nationalist Wolfe Tone attempts suicide by cutting his throat on the day of his execution and dies seven days later on 19 November*

❦ 13 ❧

1831 *The order of the Sisters of Mercy is established by Catherine McAuley*

❦ 14 ❧

Neighbours bring comfort in adversity but only envy in success
Irish proverb

Adieu to Belashanny, where I was bred and born;
Go where I may I'll think of you, as sure as night and morn

The Winding Banks of Erne, William Allingham

November ❖ Samhain

❋ 15 ❋

1985 *The governments of the Republic of Ireland and the United Kingdom sign the Anglo-Irish Agreement*

❋ 16 ❋

1986 *Death of Siobhán McKenna, Irish actress*

❋ 17 ❋

1974 *Death of Erskine Childers, fourth president of Ireland*

November ❖ Samhain

❦ 18 ❦

1967 *A statue of Wolfe Tone is unveiled at St Stephen's Green, Dublin*

❦ 19 ❦

1900 *Birth of Pamela Hinkson, Irish writer and daughter of the poet Katharine Tynan*

❦ 20 ❦

Marriages are all happy; it's having breakfast together that causes all the trouble
Irish proverb

❦ 21 ❦

1887 *Birth of Joseph Plunkett, one of the leaders of the 1916 Rising*

November ⬧ Samhain

✣ 22 ✣

1963 *American President John F. Kennedy is assassinated in Dallas, Texas*

✣ 23 ✣

The best way to get rid of your enemies is God's way, by loving them
Irish proverb

✣ 24 ✣

1922 *IRA member Robert Erskine Childers is shot by the Free State Army for illegally carrying a firearm*

✣ 25 ✣

1906 *Birth of Sadie Paterson, Irish trade unionist and peace activist*

✣ 26 ✣

1794 *First Irish convicts arrive in New South Wales, Australia*

✣ 27 ✣

1871 *The Gaiety Theatre opens in Dublin*

✣ 28 ✣

1969 *Birth of Sonia O'Sullivan, Olympic athlete, in Cobh, Co. Cork*

Blessings too, my love on you, a-sleeping and awakening

Ellen Brown, J. C. Mangan

❉ 29 ❉

1898 *C.S. Lewis, author of* The Chronicles of Narnia, *is born in Belfast*

❉ 30 ❉

1995 *President Clinton is the first American president to visit Northern Ireland*

DECEMBER
NOLLAIG

DECEMBER ❖ NOLLAIG

❧ 1 ❧
1495 *Edward Poyning, Henry VII's Lord Deputy in Ireland, issues a declaration, known as Poyning's Law, under which the Irish parliament could no longer pass any laws without the prior consent of the English parliament*

❧ 2 ❧
1811 *The Kildare Place Society is founded to organise non-denominational schools in Ireland*

❧ 3 ❧
1990 *Mary Robinson begins to serve as the first female president of Ireland, until 12 September 1997*

❧ 4 ❧
You can take a man out of the bog, but you can't take the bog out of the man
Irish proverb

❧ 5 ❧
1947 *Birth of Tony Gregory (d. 2009), Irish independent politician and TD for Dublin Central 1982–2009*

❧ 6 ❧
1921 *The Anglo-Irish Treaty is signed, creating the Irish Free State, coming into force in 1922*

❧ 7 ❧
Come home with me, I want to introduce you to my mother. We have founded a society for the suppression of Virtue
Oscar Wilde

Her hair behold it does shine like gold
And is finely rolled and so nicely grows

The Star of Slane, street ballad

December ❖ Nollaig

✿ 8 ✿

Soft words butter no parsnips but they won't harden the heart of the cabbage either
Irish proverb

✿ 9 ✿

1973 *The Sunningdale Agreement is signed in Belfast by British, Irish and Northern Ireland representatives*

✿ 10 ✿

1998 *John Hume and David Trimble receive the Nobel Peace Prize*

✿ 11 ✿

1872 *Birth of René Bull, Irish illustrator (d. 1942)*

✿ 12 ✿

1928 *Issue of the Irish Free State currency*

✿ 13 ✿

1971 *Birth of Naomi Long MP, second female lord mayor of Belfast (served 2009–2010)*

✿ 14 ✿

1831 *In what became known as the Carrickshock Incident, 17 people are killed in a riot after efforts to serve tithe summons on Irish peasants*

How oft I dream of thee

O Arranmore, loved Arranmore, Tom Moore

December ◆ Nollaig

15

1930 *Birth of Irish novelist Edna O'Brien*

16

1955 *The Republic of Ireland joins the United Nations together with 16 other sovereign states*

17

1834 *The world's first suburban railway line, from Dublin to Dún Laoghaire, opens*

18

I should imagine that most mothers don't quite understand their sons
Oscar Wilde

DECEMBER ❖ NOLLAIG

❈❧ 19 ❧❈

1973 *The Irish Supreme Court rules to overturn the prohibition on the importation of contraceptives*

❈❧ 20 ❧❈

1909 *The Volta, Ireland's first cinema, opens in Dublin*

❈❧ 21 ❧❈

She would drink the cream and say the cat she had was an old rogue
Irish proverb

I would to tell to all around me how my fondness grew

Róisín Dubh, Thomas Furlong

December ❖ Nollaig

❋ 22 ❋

1989 *Death of Samuel Beckett in Paris, aged 83*

❋ 23 ❋

1958 *Death of Dorothy McArdle, Irish writer and nationalist*

❋ 24 ❋

1946 *Government Departments of Health and Social Welfare are established in the Republic of Ireland*

Have I not called thee angel-like and fair?

Two sonnets to Caroline, J. C. Mangan

ETATIS · SVÆ · 34 ·

DECEMBER ❖ NOLLAIG

❧ 25 ❧

1916 460 Irish 1916 Rising prisoners are released by the British Government

Where glows the Irish hearth with peat,
There lives a subtle spell

Cois na Teineadh, T. W. Rolleston

December ❖ Nollaig

🌿 26 🌿
1916 *Birth of Kathleen O'Flaherty, Irish writer and academic*

🌿 27 🌿
1904 *Opening of the Abbey Theatre in Dublin*

🌿 28 🌿
1937 *The Irish Constitution becomes law at midnight*

🌿 29 🌿
1937 *The Constitution of Ireland comes into force, replacing the Irish Free State with a new state called 'Éire', or, in the English language, 'Ireland'*

🌿 30 🌿
1759 *Arthur Guinness signs a 9,000-year lease for the St James's Gate brewery*

🌿 31 🌿
In the New Year, may your right hand always be stretched out in friendship, never in want
Irish saying

Why has music power to melt?
Oh! because it speaks like thee.

Comparisons, T. Moore

PICTURE CREDITS